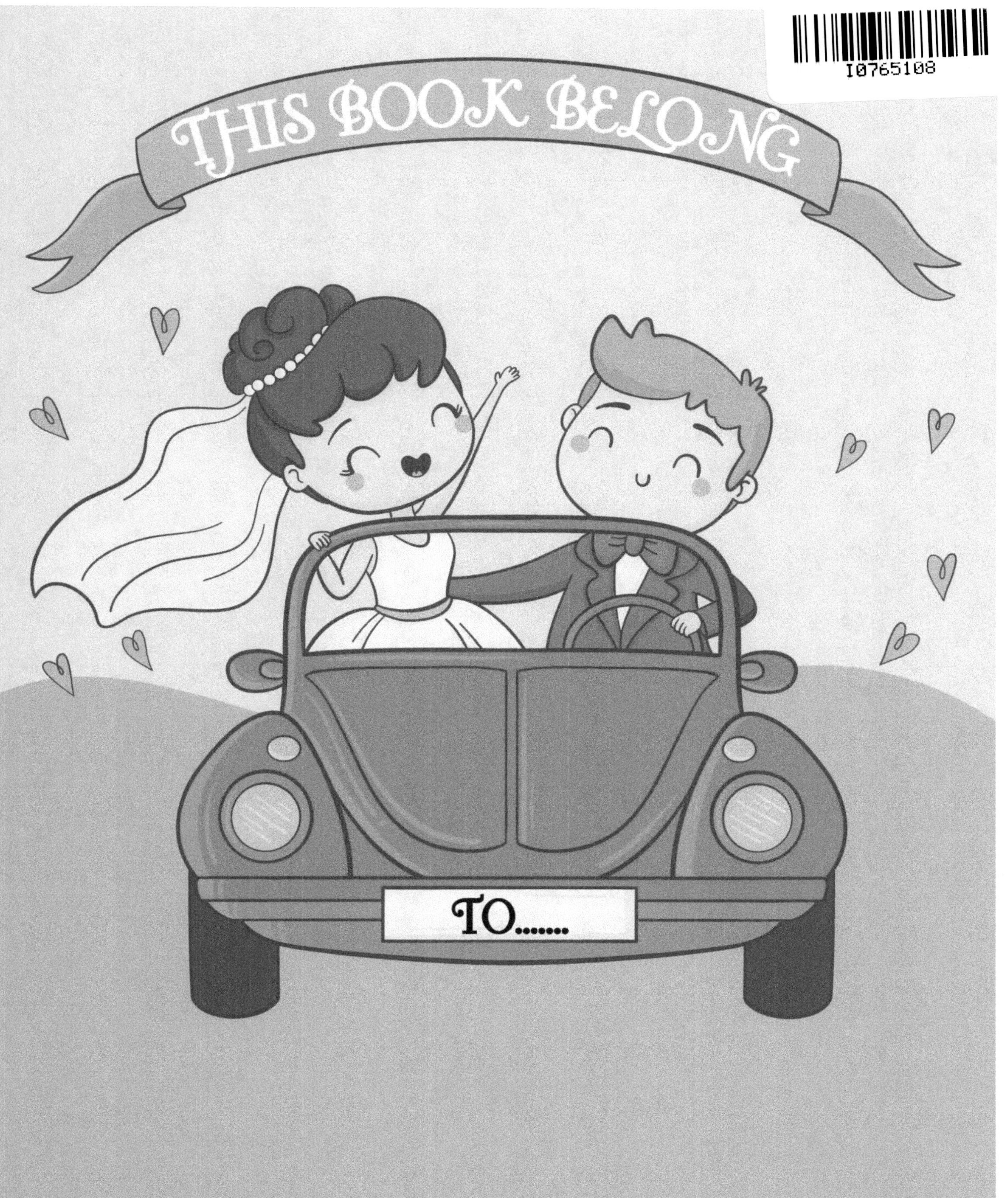

THIS BOOK BELONG
TO........
I0765108

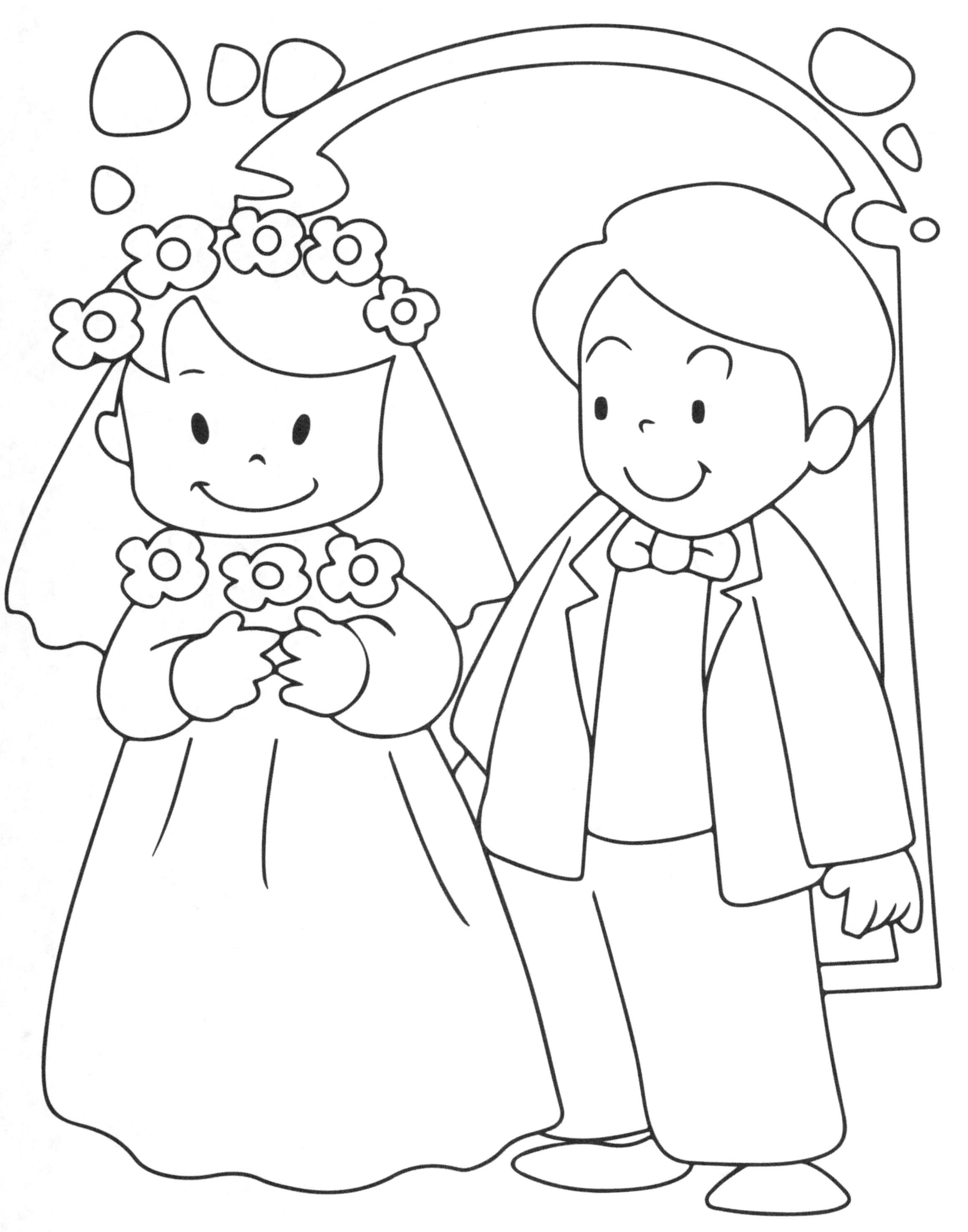

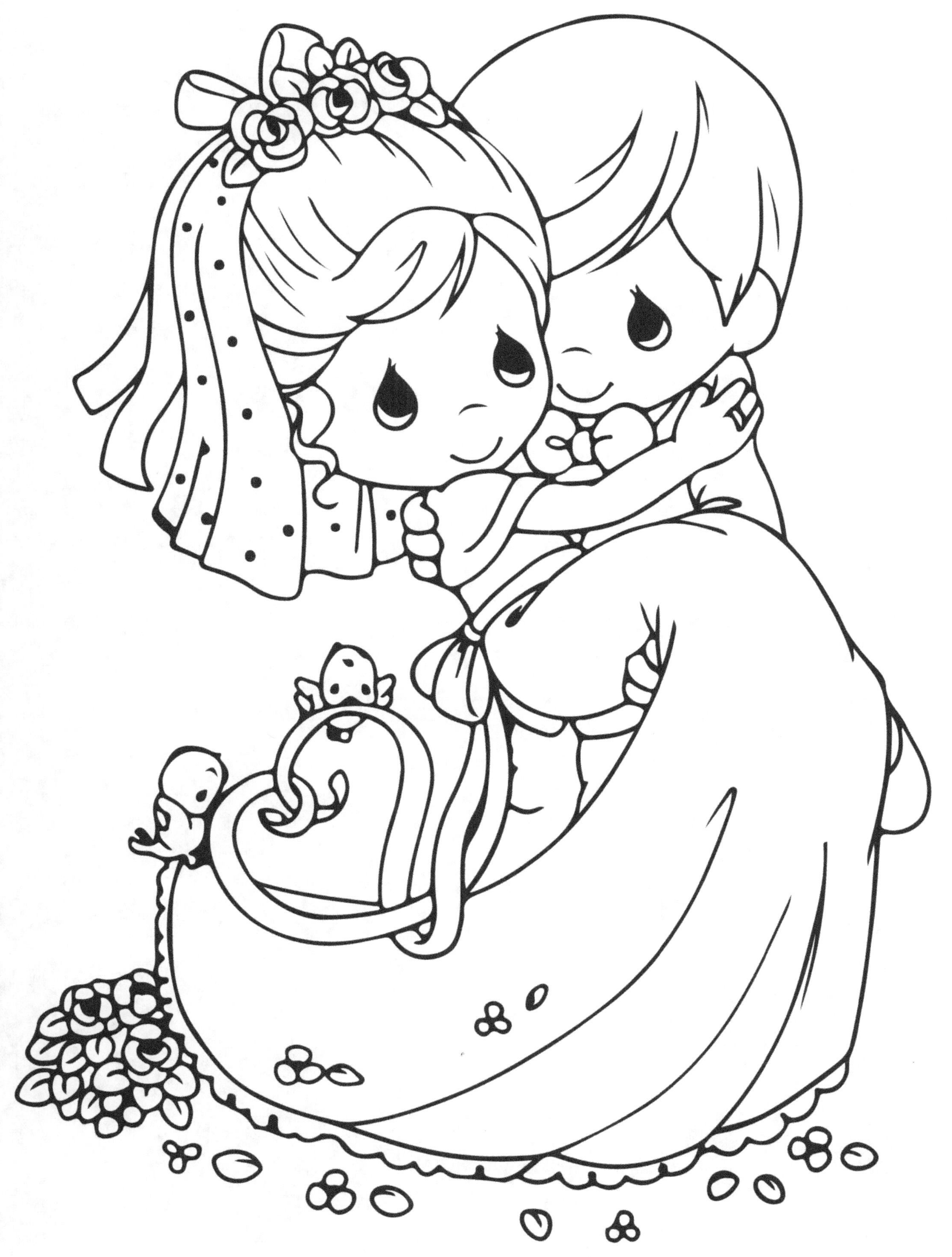

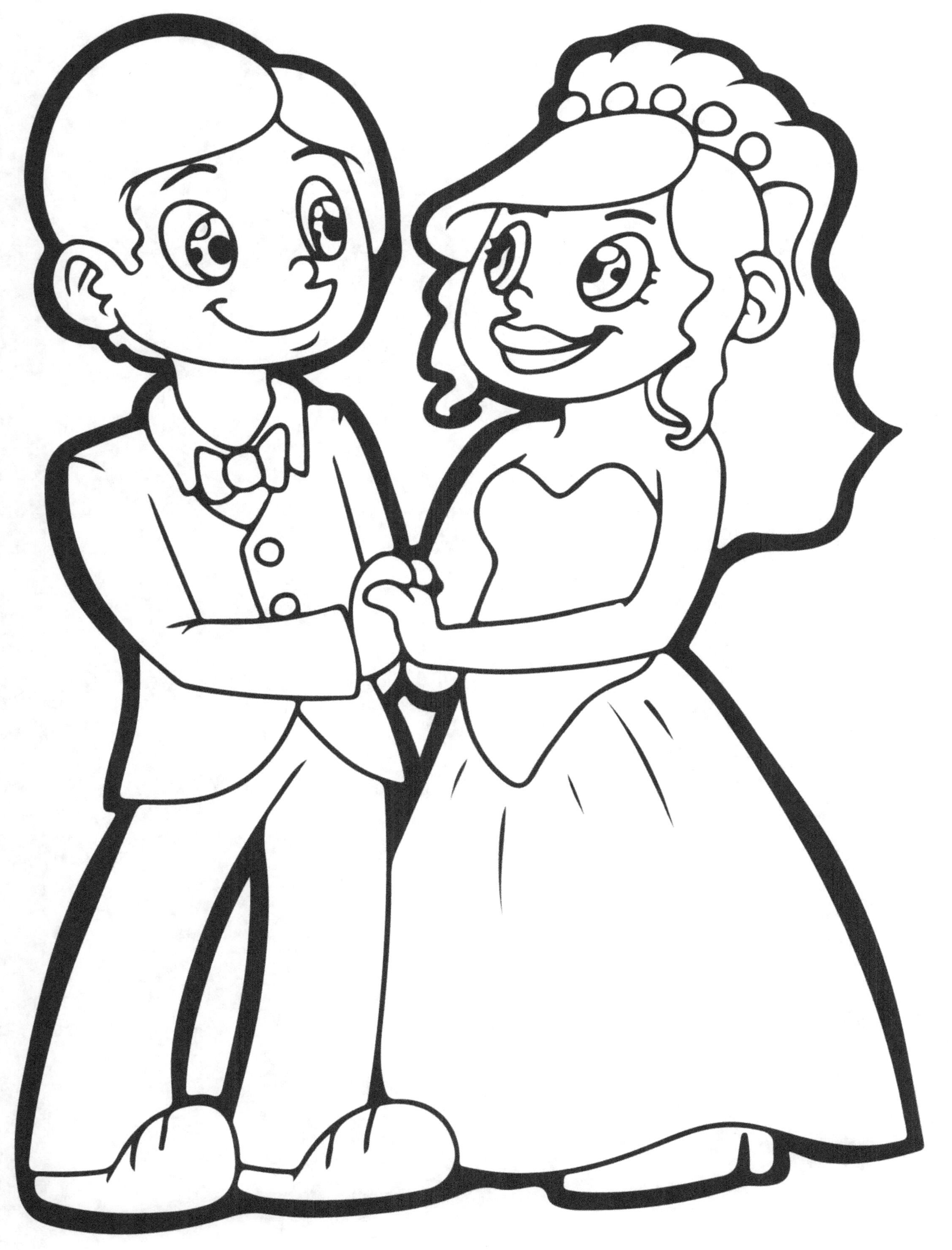

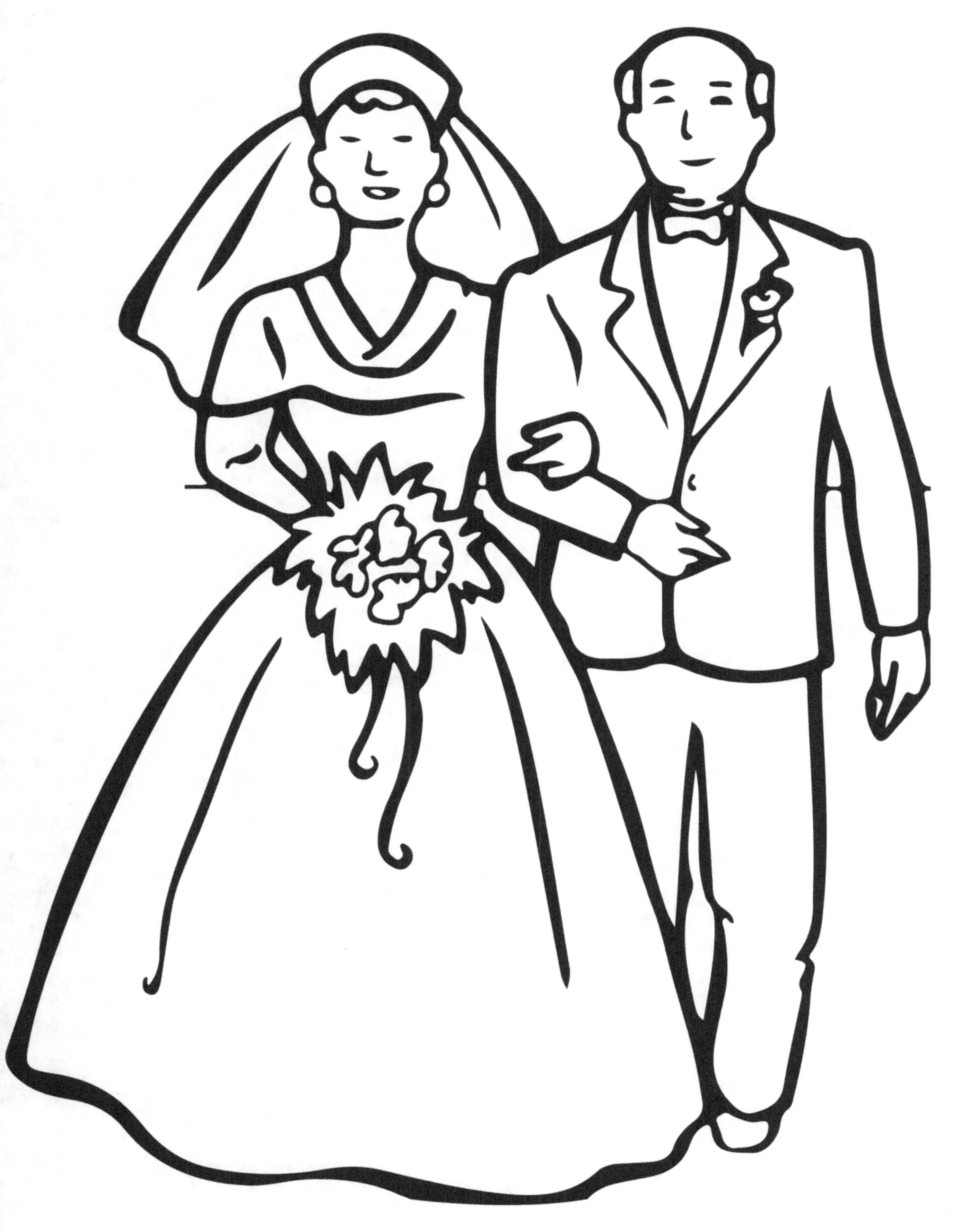

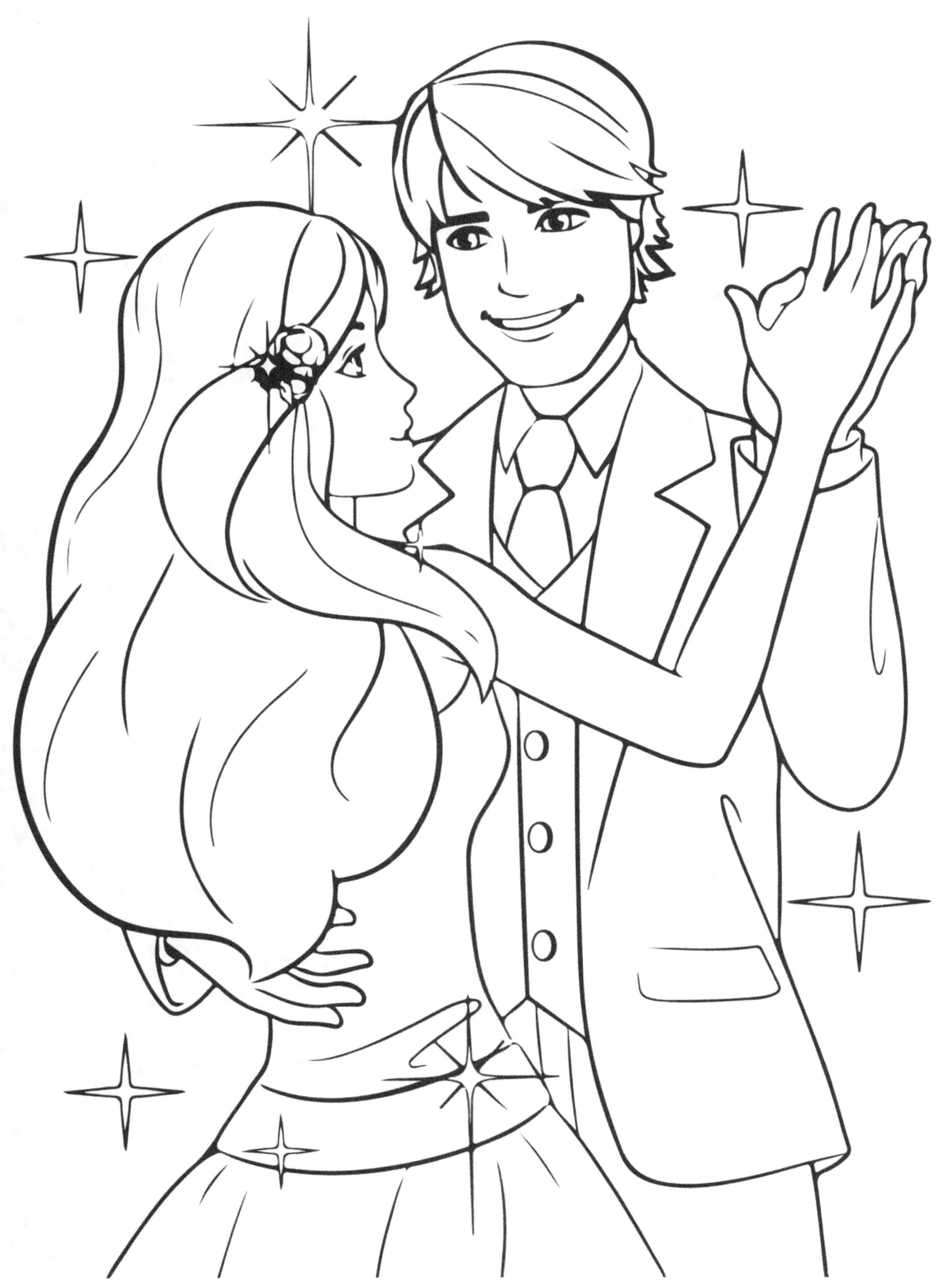

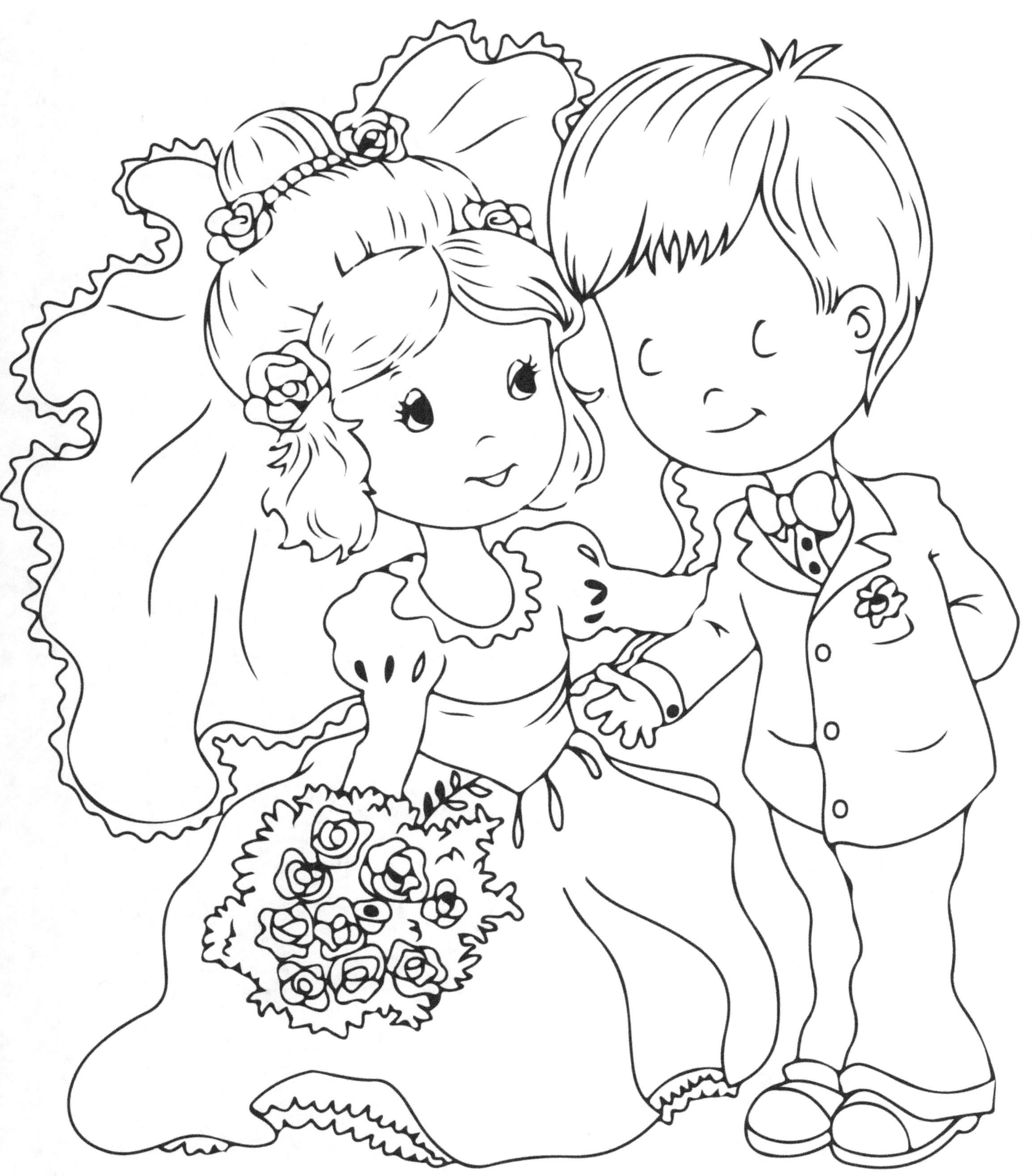

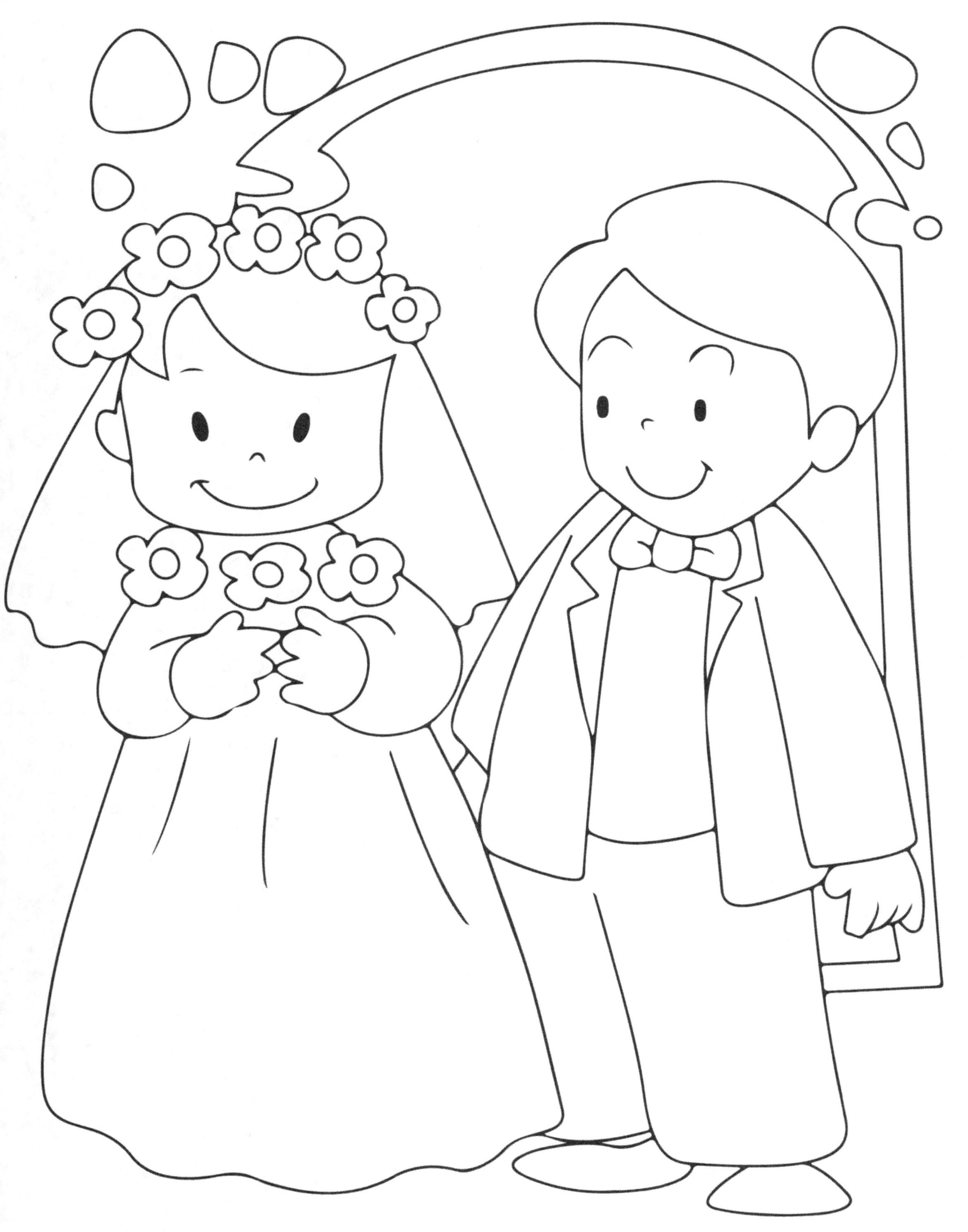

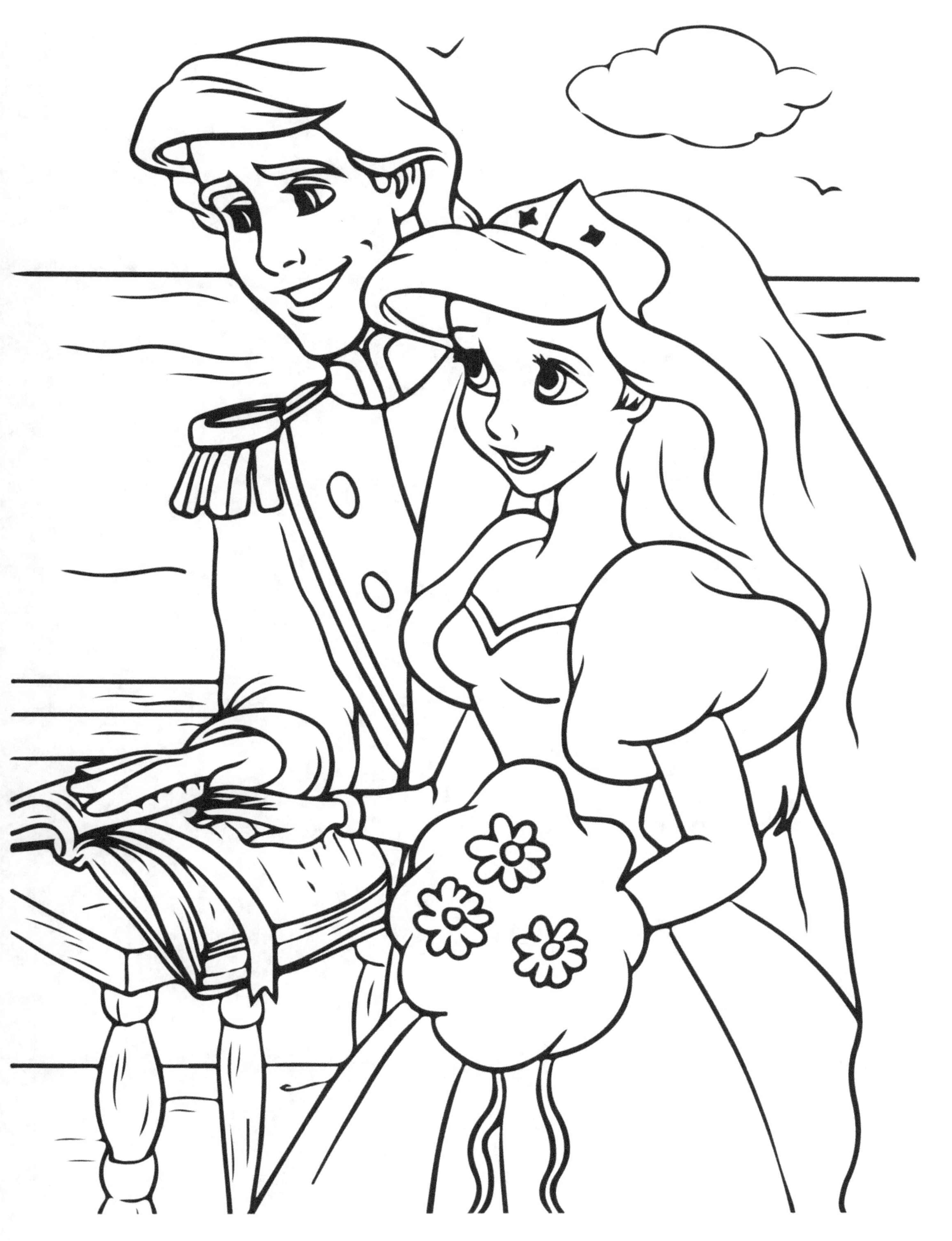

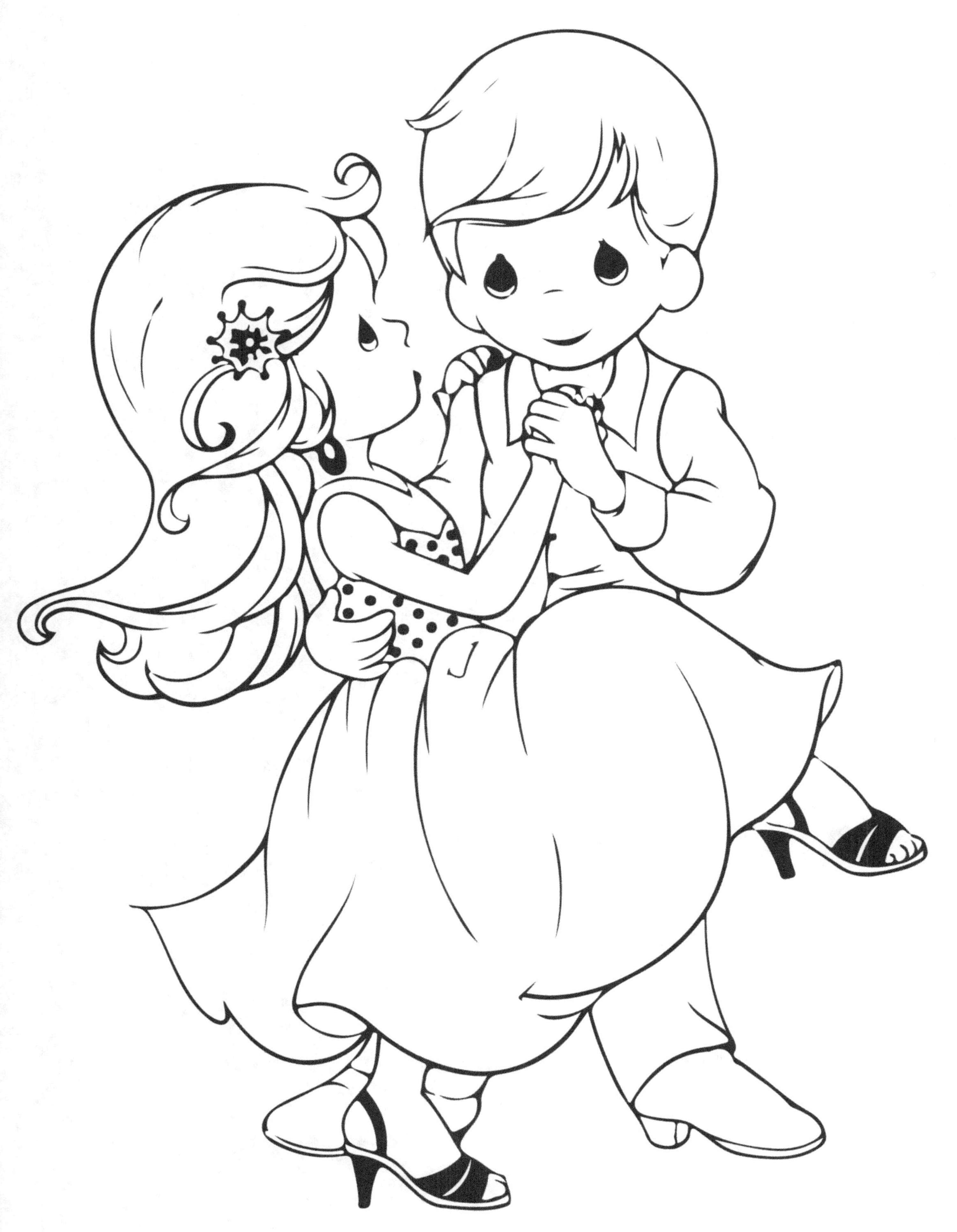

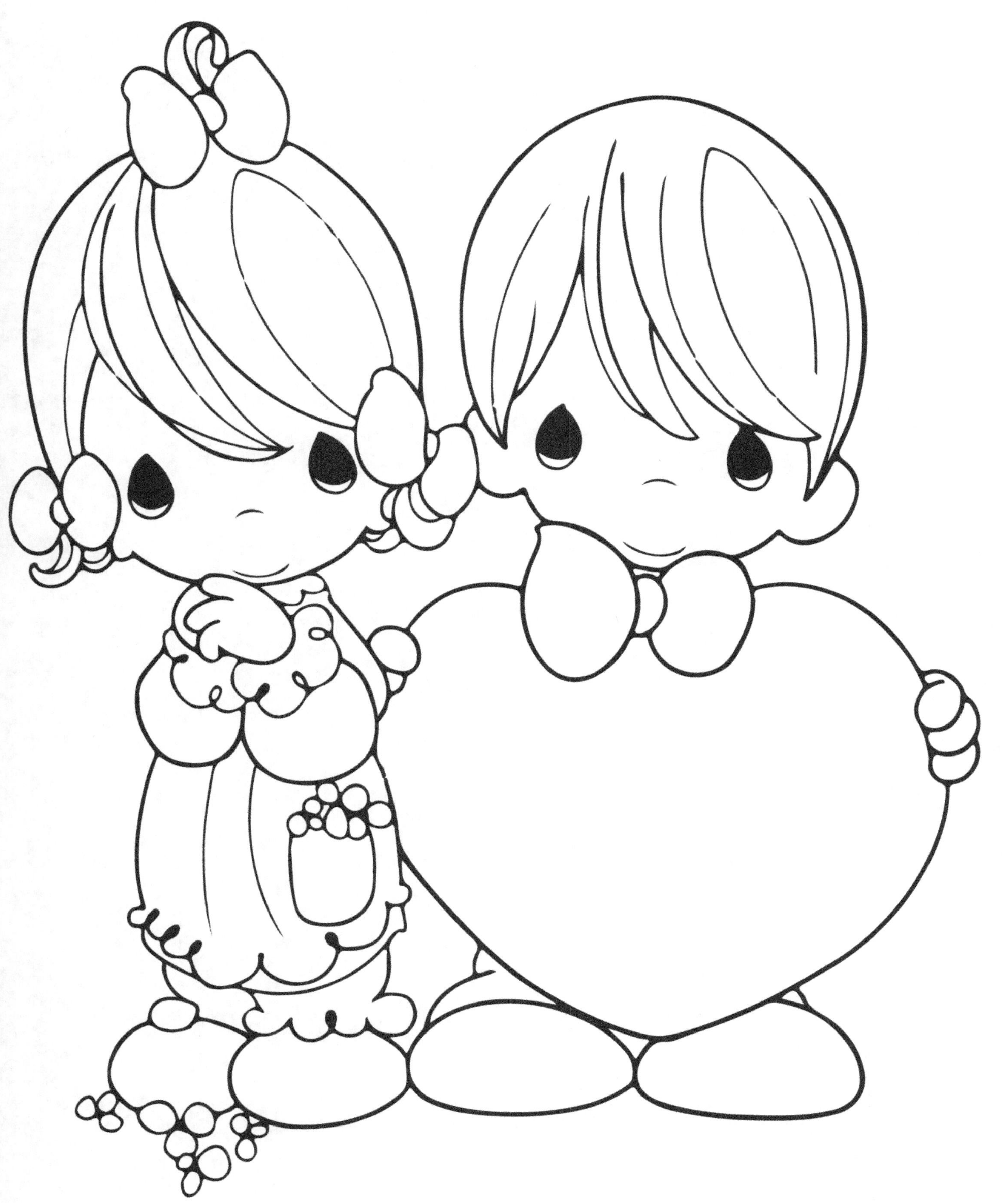

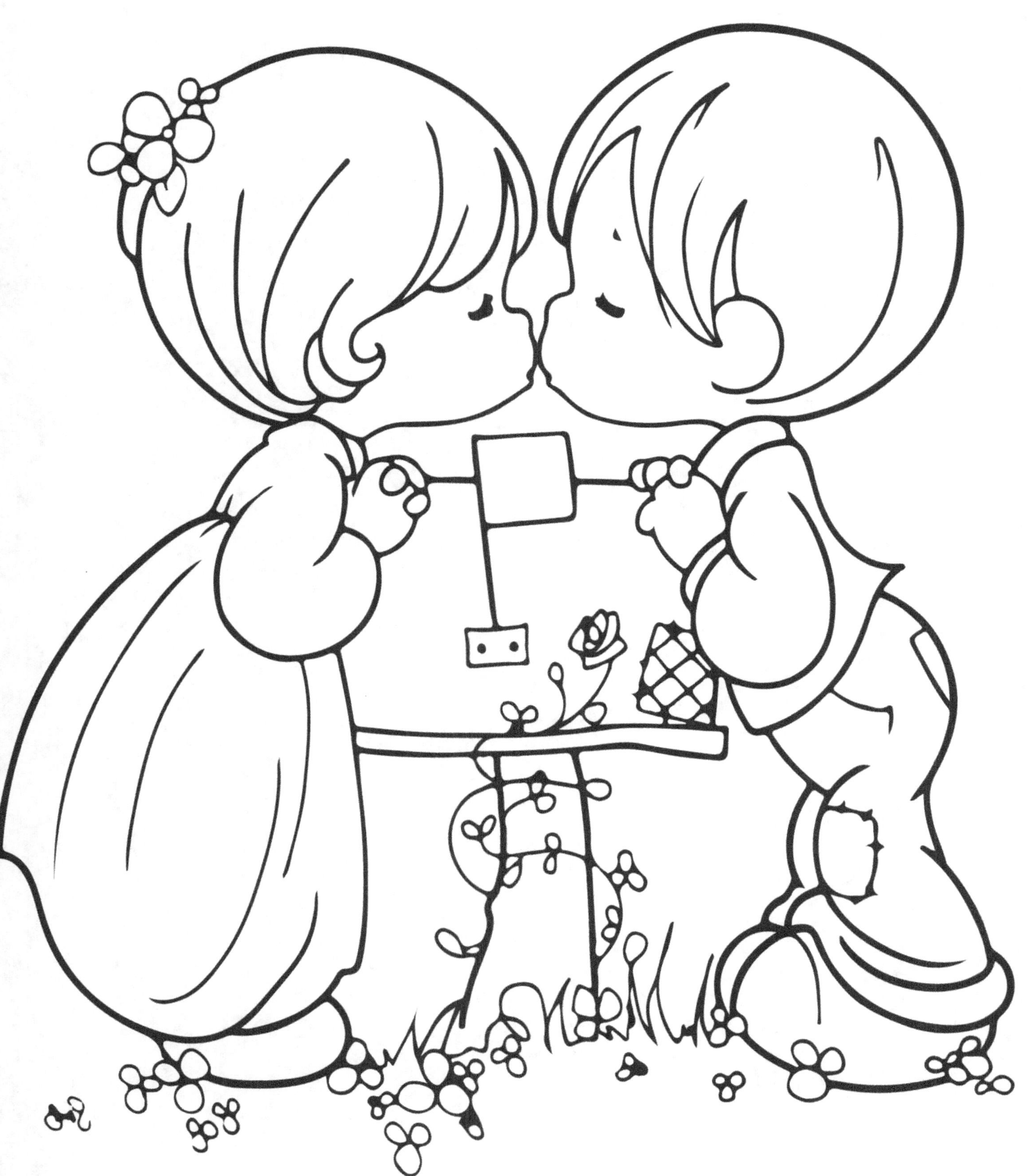

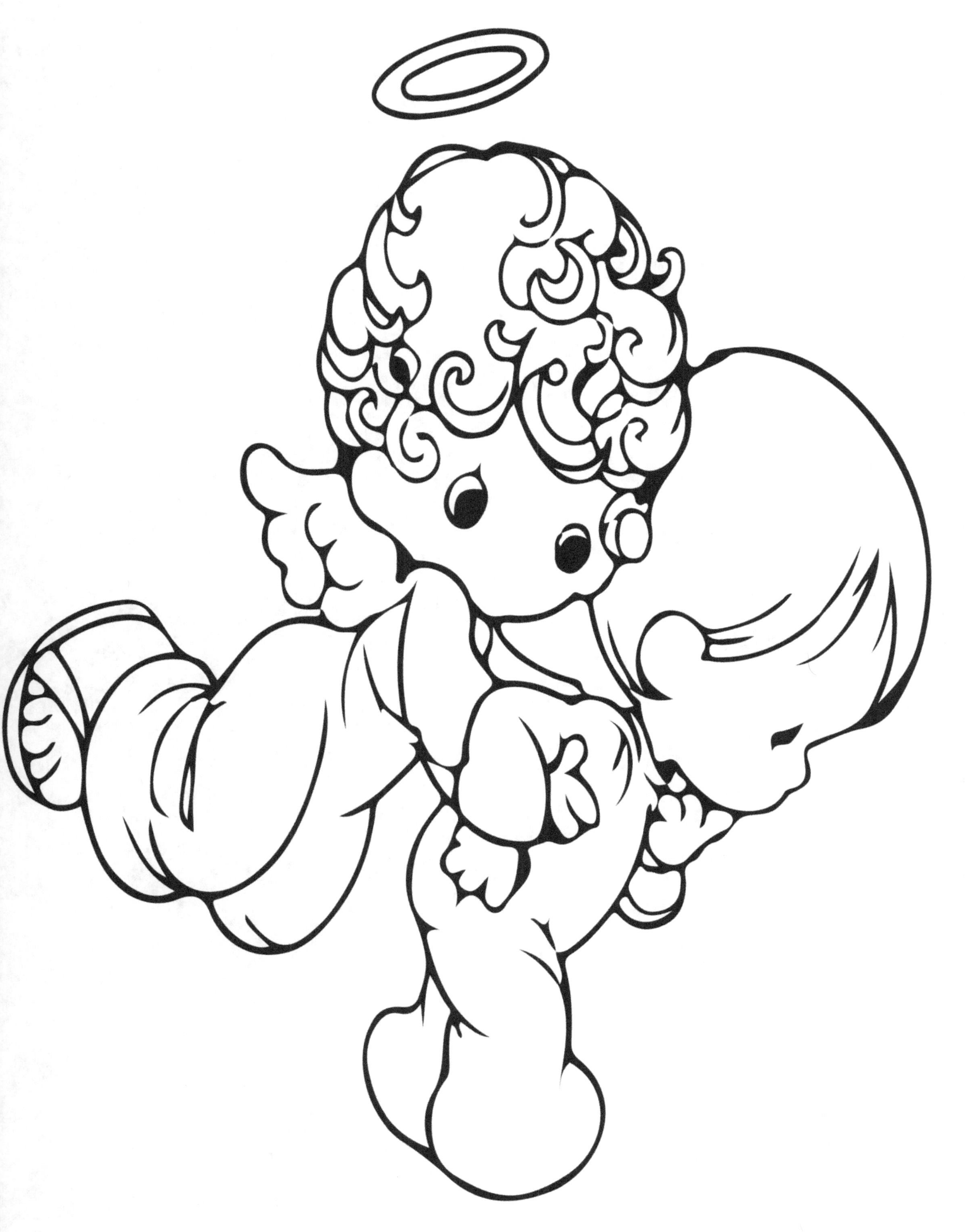

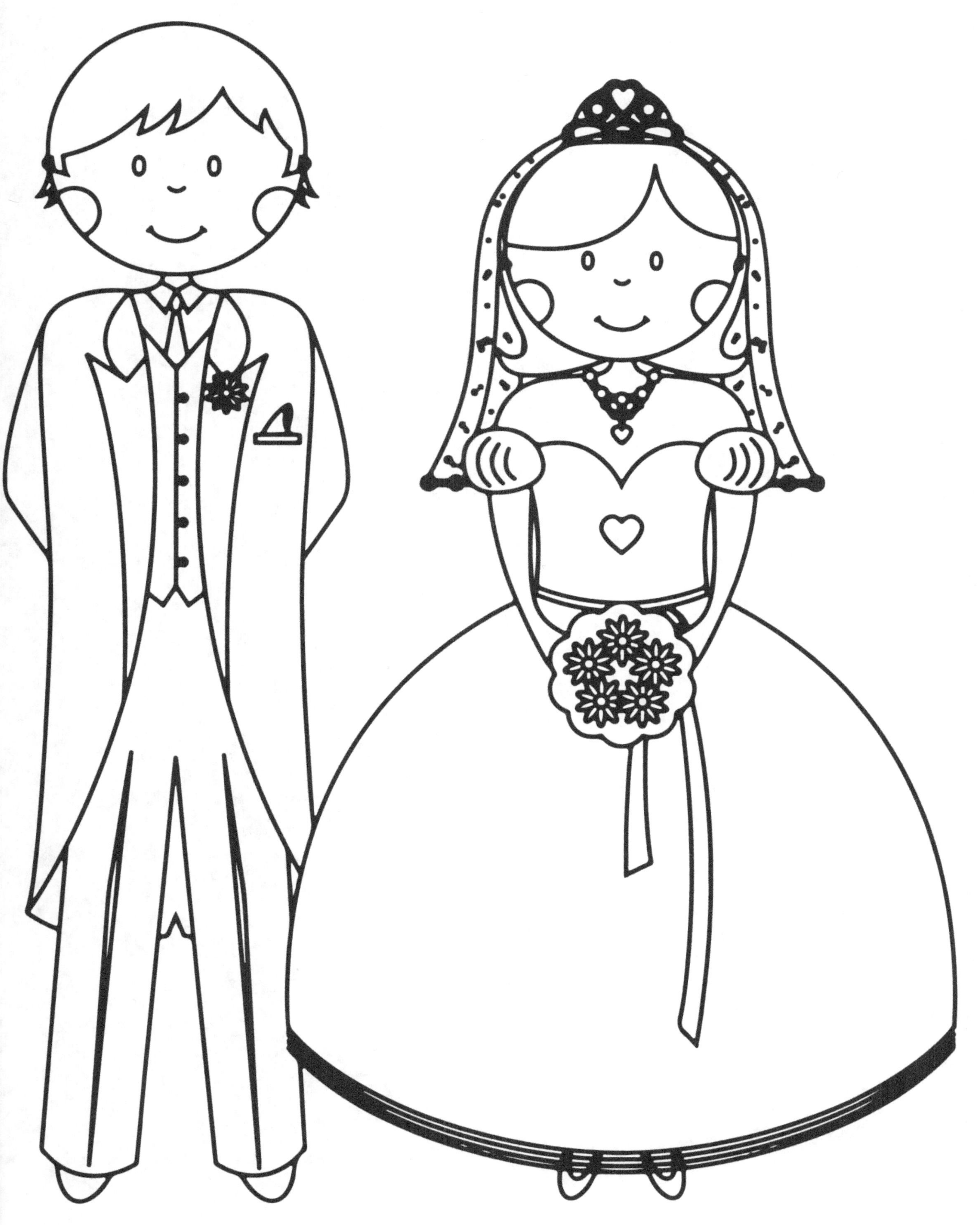

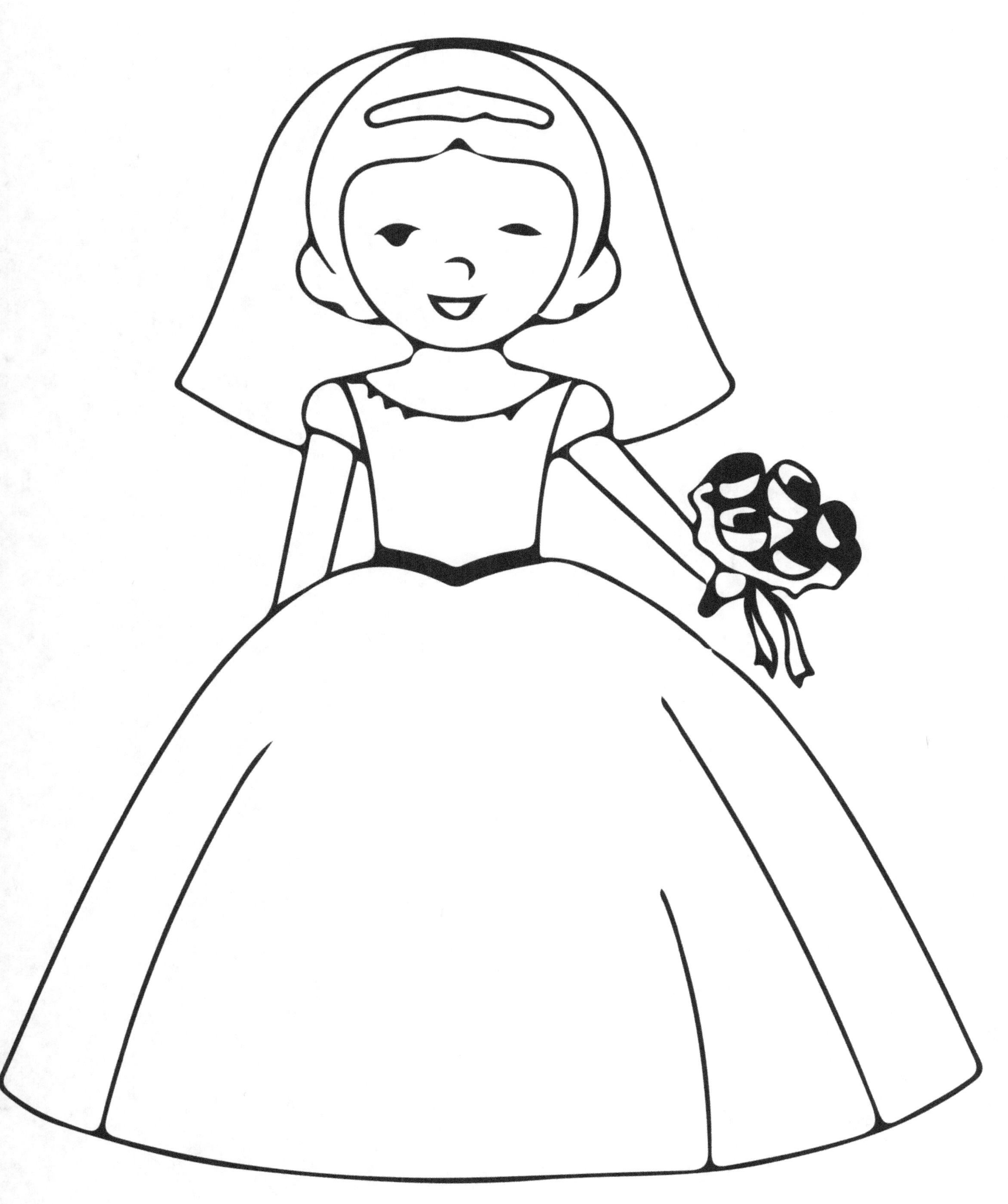

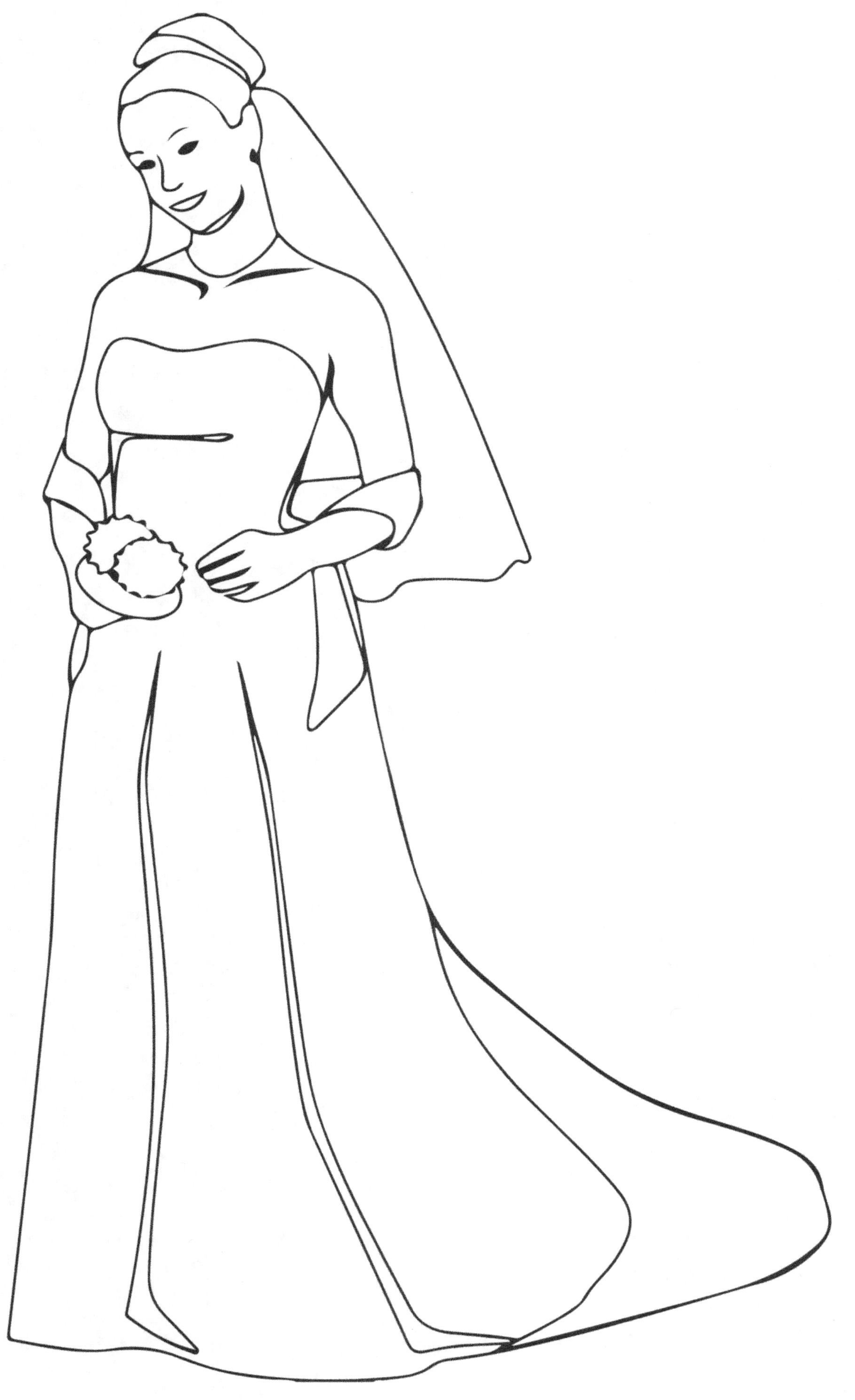

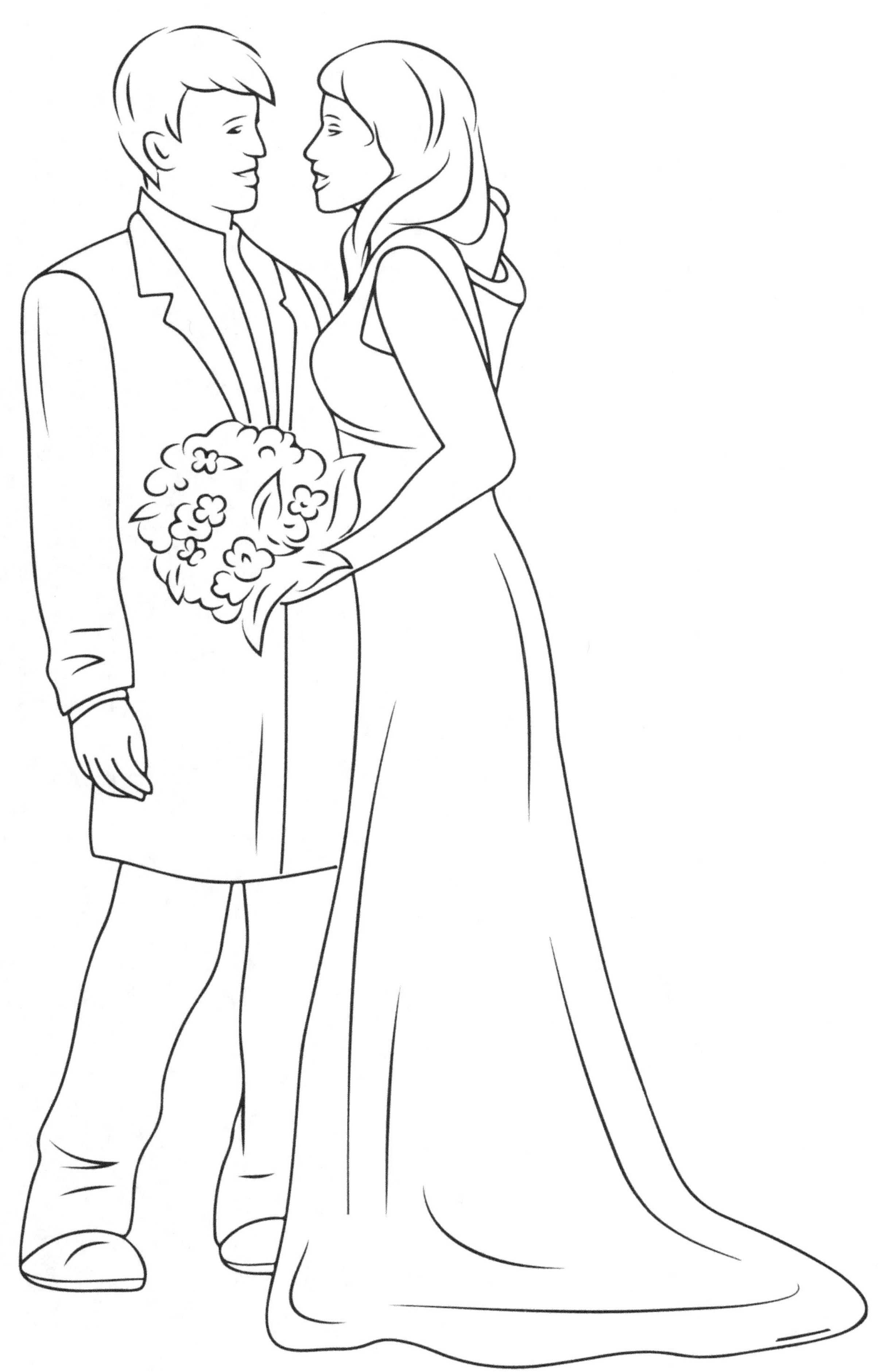

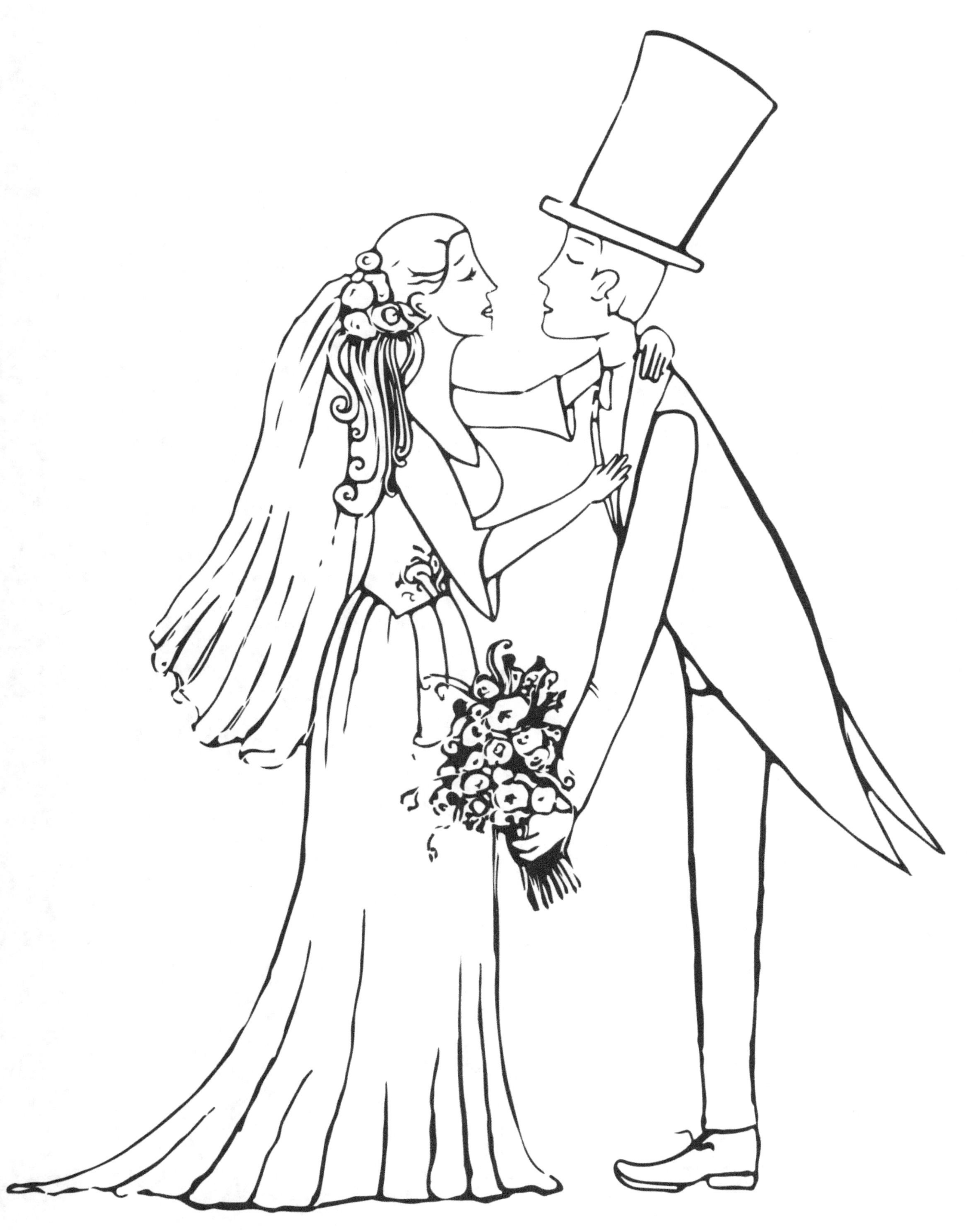

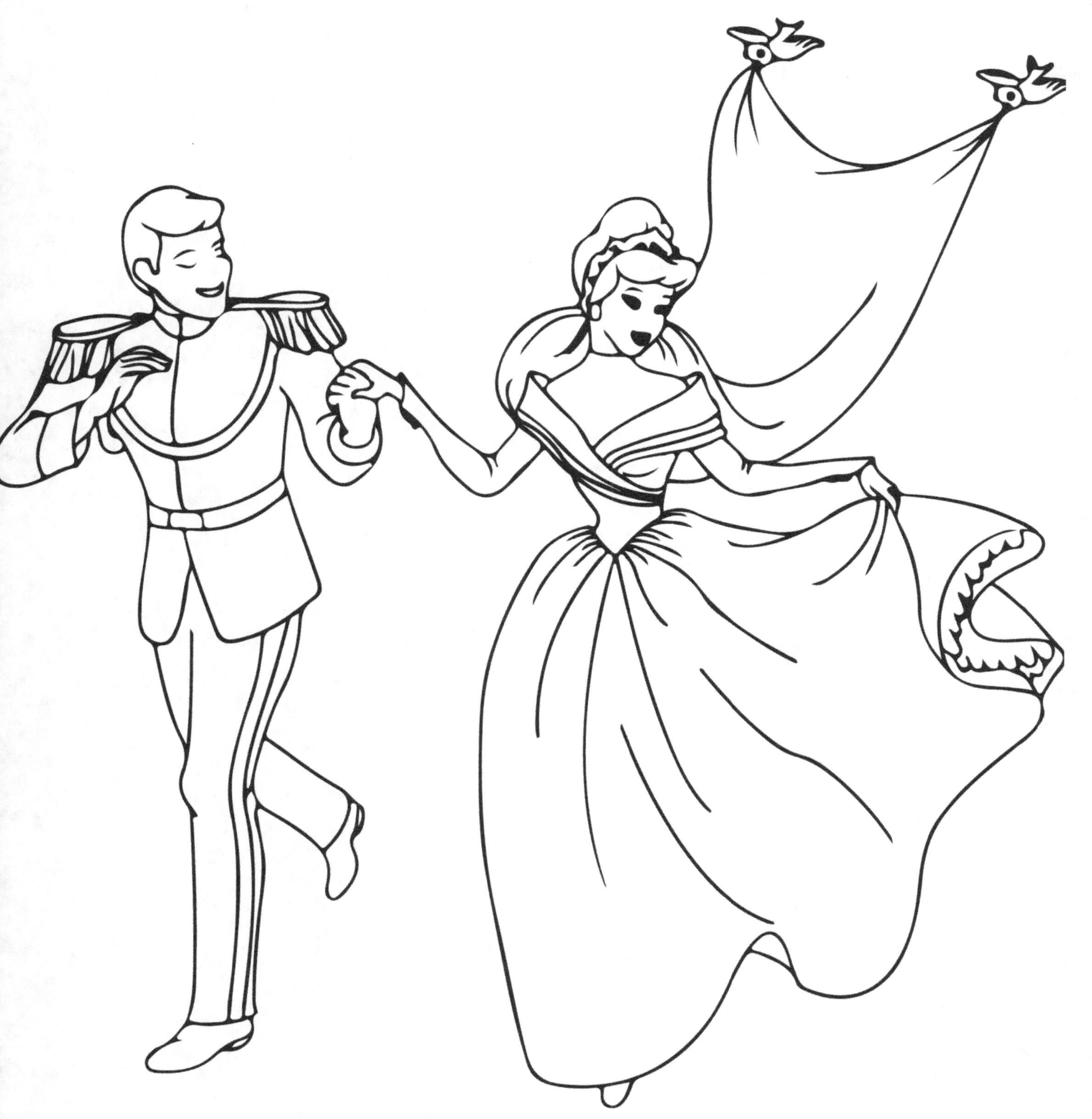

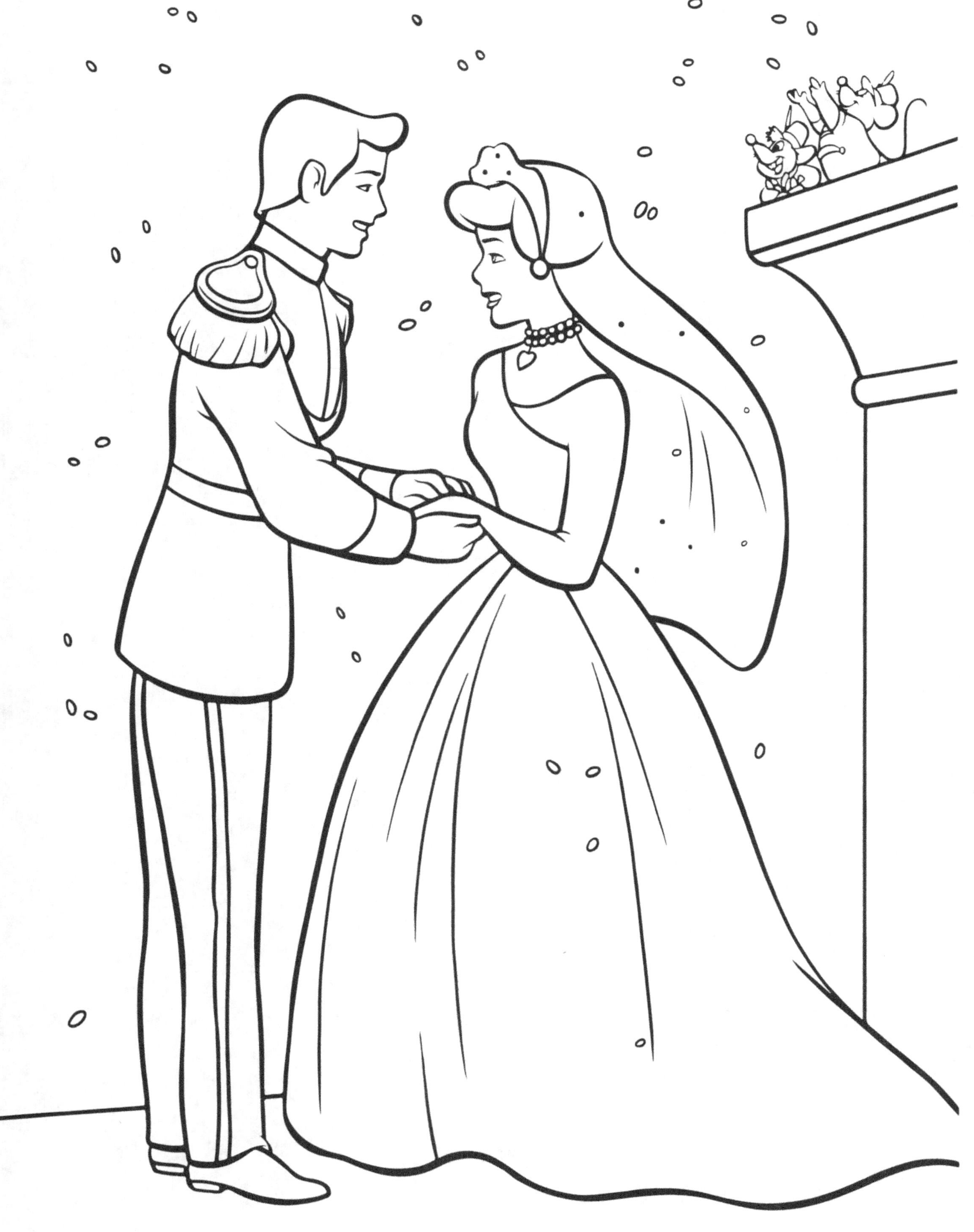

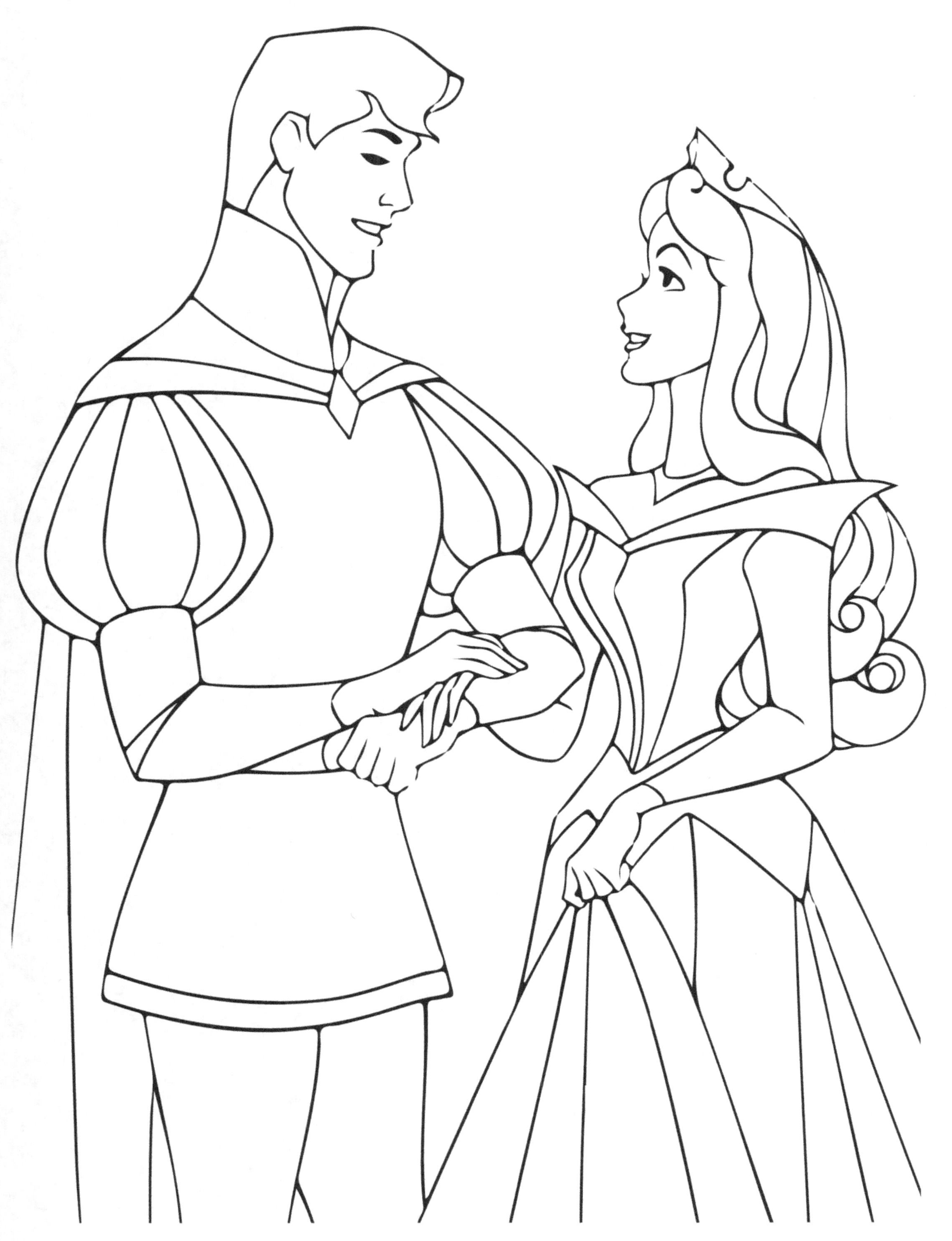

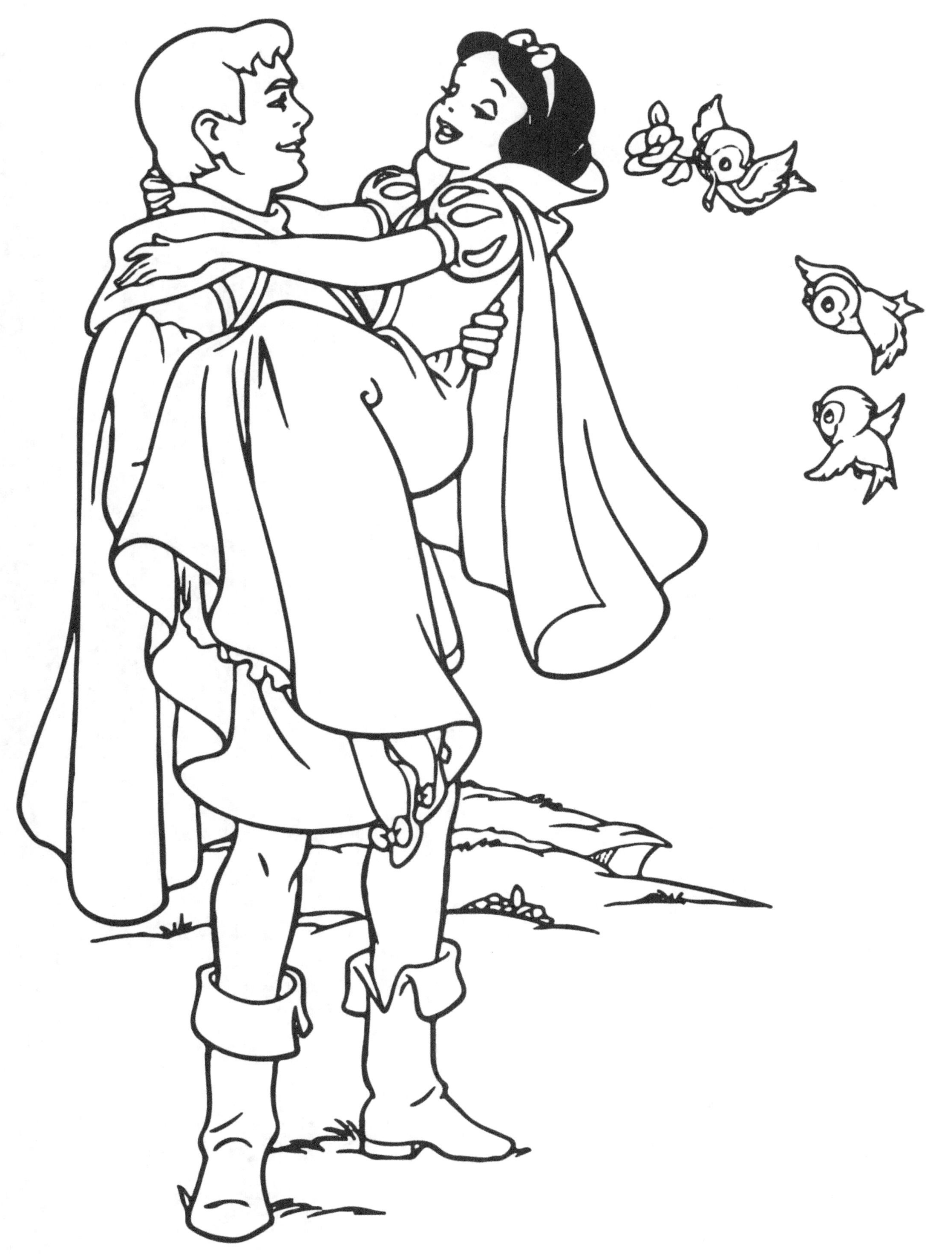

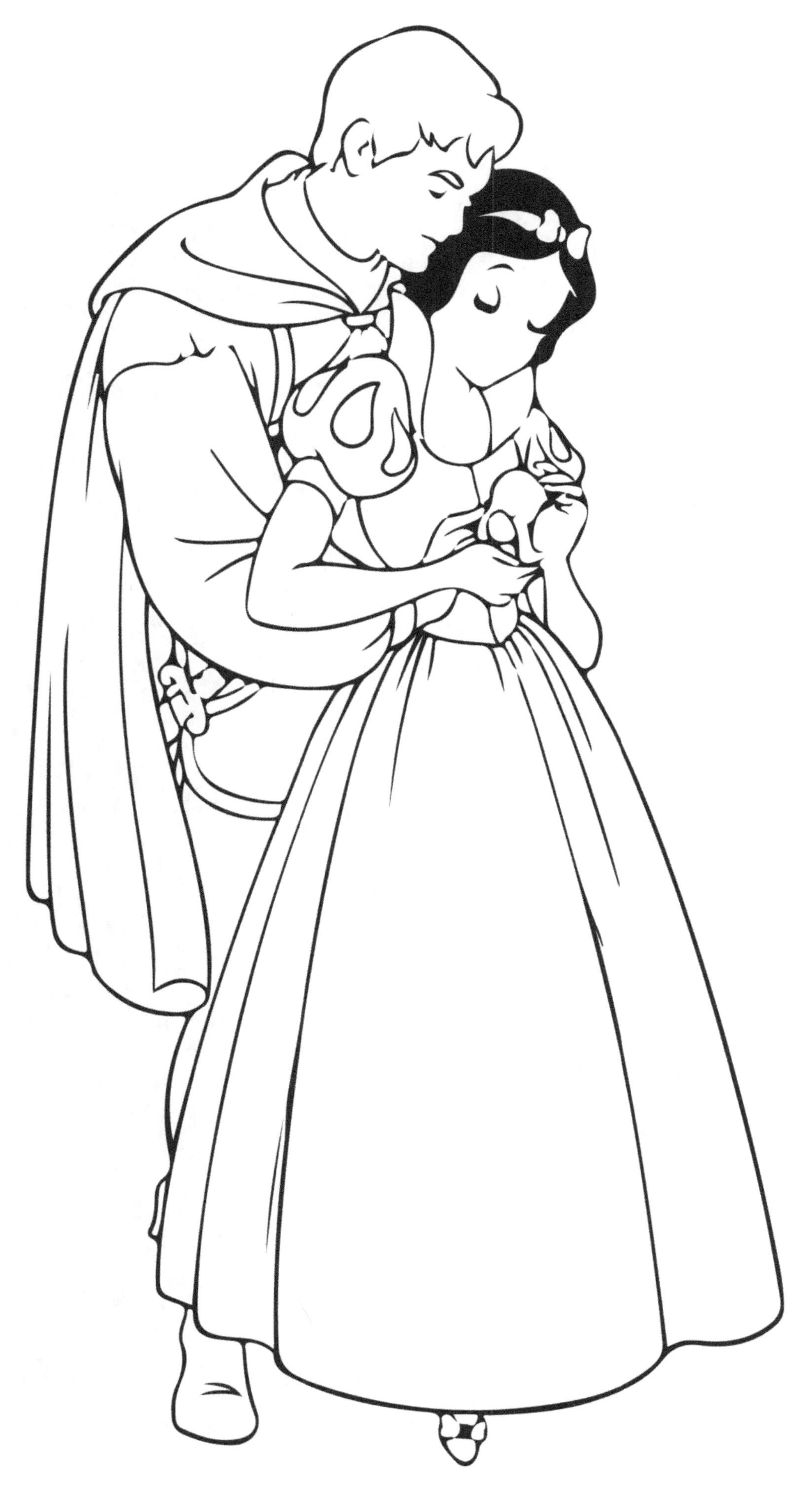

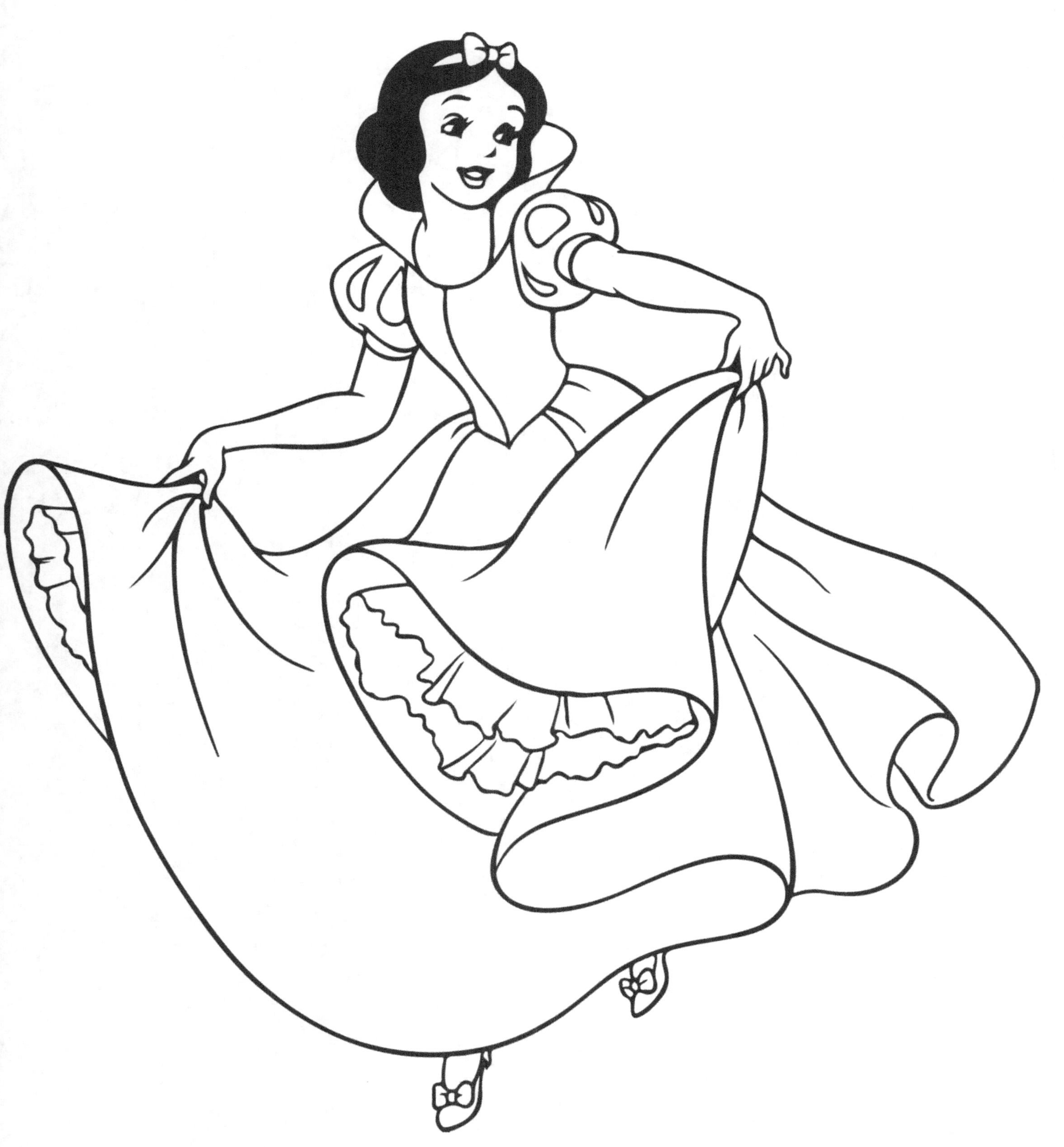

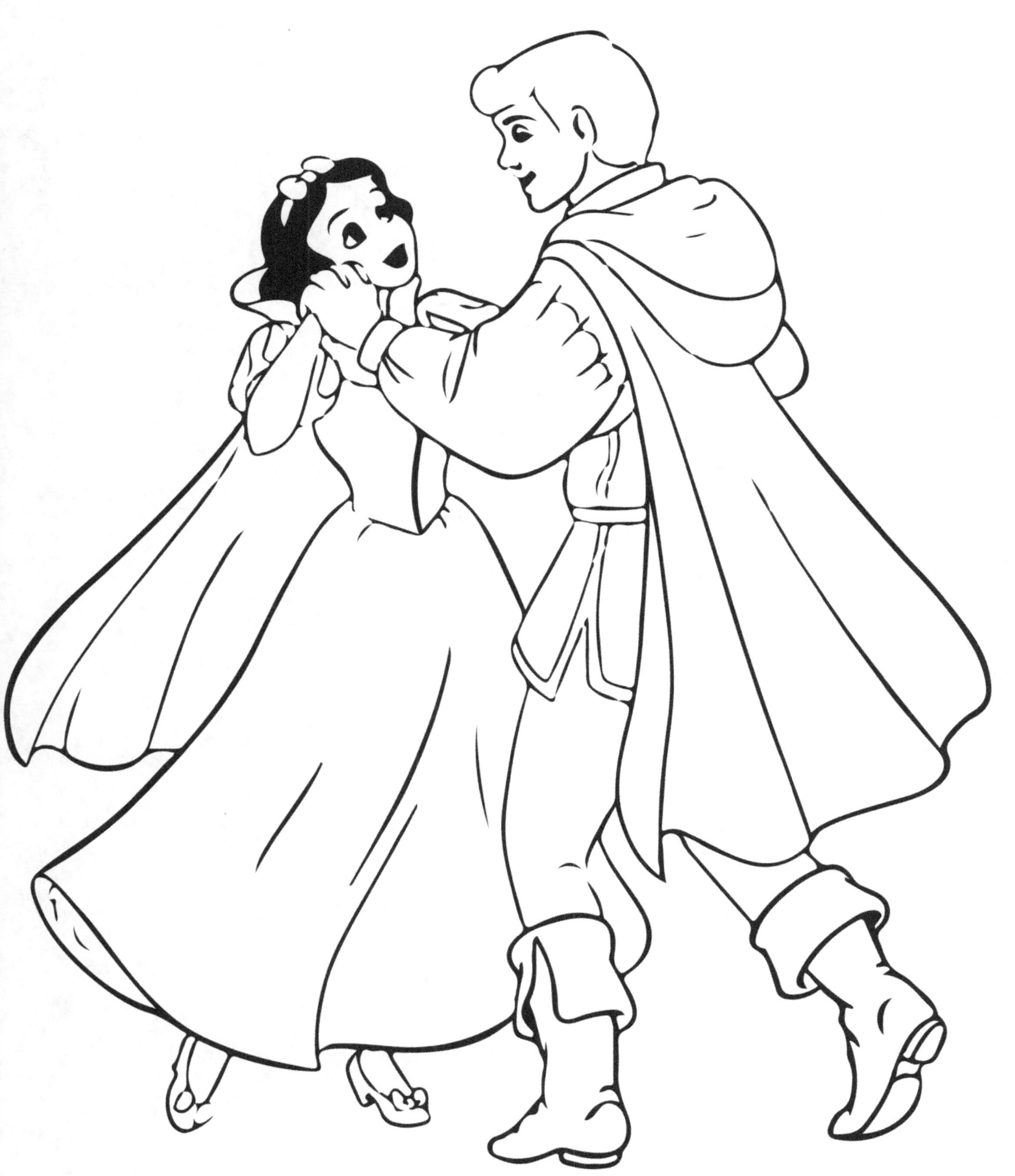